DAISY RIDLEY

Rey Forever

DAISY RIDLEY

Rey Forever
BY EmilyPullman

FILM STARS

Volume 2

STAR WARS
EDITION

creative
media
Publishing

CREATIVE MEDIA, INC.
PO Box 6270
Whittier, California 90609-6270
United States of America

Book & cover design by Joseph Dzidrums

www.creativemedia.net

First Edition: May 2017

LCCN: On File
ISBN 978-1-938438-60-8
eISBN: 978-1-938438-61-5

FOR
THE DREAM

TABLE OF CONTENTS

"I think I've been very lucky in my life to be able to look up to incredible women."

Daisy Jazz Isobel Ridley was born in Westminster, England, on April 10, 1992. Her parents are named Louise Fawkner-Corbett and Christopher Ridley. Louise works as a publicity manager at a bank, and Christopher is an accomplished photographer.

Daisy has two older sisters, Kika-Rose Ridley (b. 1989), and Poppy Sophia Ridley (b. 1986). Kika-Rose is a model with top agency Models 1, and Poppy Sophia is an aspiring musician. The actress also has two half-sisters from her father's first marriage.

When Daisy was growing up, the Ridleys lived in an exclusive part of central London. The large family resided in a five-bedroom mews house. Built in the 18th and 19th century, a mews home was originally constructed to house horses, but in recent years, it has become a stylish 21st century home.

As a young girl, Daisy repeatedly watched the 1996 movie *Matilda* starring Mara Wilson, Danny DeVito, and Rhea Perlman. Based on the classic Roald Dahl children's book, the whimsical story follows a four-year-old prodigy with neglectful parents who survives life by teaching herself how to read. Along the way, she also discovers a talent for telekinesis, the ability to move items through mind power.

"I aspired to be like (Matilda)," Daisy told Carrie Fisher in a profile piece for *Interview* magazine. "I wanted to be a girl who could make a jug of water tip into a glass."

While growing up, Daisy hoped to work with monkeys when she reached adulthood. An animal lover, she dreamed of becoming a zoologist. Never did she fantasize about being an actress.

After discovering their daughter could carry a tune, Daisy's parents enrolled her in singing lessons. Shortly afterward, she showed a flair for the dramatics, too. The talented girl could also dance well, establishing herself as a triple threat.

At age nine, Daisy auditioned for Tring Park School for the Performing Arts, an institution that offered an exceptional academic education while also training young students in acting, dance, musical theater, and commercial music. The youngster's tryout thoroughly impressed the admissions board, and they offered the talented girl a full scholarship to the school.

Daisy's mother and father felt thrilled when the prestigious school welcomed their daughter with open arms. They long believed that the rambunctious youth possessed an excessive amount of endless energy. The parents hoped their daughter would thrive in a bustling, challenging environment that kept her busy but still provided her with a top-notch education.

Daisy focused on her scholastic studies while she also trained as an actress at the school until the age of 18. A natural entertainer, she flourished in the musical theater program, belting out demanding show tunes with enviable ease. The determined adolescent consistently impressed teachers by working hard and never settling for second best.

As a performing arts school, it was no surprise that Tring Park often produced quality theatrical shows. At the age of sixteen, Daisy felt thrilled to be a part of the school's production of the musical *Crazy for You*. The teenager enjoyed appearing in the Tony-Award winning romantic comedy featuring the popular songs of George and Ira Gershwin.

When Daisy was seventeen years old, she won the part of polite Nancy in her school's production of Sandy Wilson's *The Boy Friend*. The flapper musical set on the French Riviera follows the love lives of several young girls attending Madame Dubonnet's Finishing School. The thrilled teenager performed in four dance numbers: "Perfect Young Ladies," "The Boy Friend," "Sur La Plage," and "The Riviera."

During the run of *The Boy Friend*, a powerful snow storm hit the Tring area. Even though Daisy lived two miles from the school, she felt the show had to go on! The plucky girl walked all the way to the theater in the snow. Some of her classmates, who lived closer to school than she did, did not even bother showing up for showtime.

Daisy's determination impressed the school faculty and all who heard about it. Not only was the young girl incredibly talented, but she was also fiercely committed to projects. Not surprisingly, the gifted student even took top honors that year by winning the

Classical Cup competition. Most people agreed that if she continued taking her craft seriously, the youngest Ridley child would be going places someday!

"Growing up I was always aware of the mythology surrounding Star Wars because it's such a pop-culture phenomenon."

After her high school graduation, Daisy attended countless auditions for various film, television, and stage projects with varying degrees of success. In 2013, she ate a pork pie in a supermarket commercial. Next, the actress played a music nerd named Jessie in *Youngers*, a British show about teenagers pursuing music careers. She also appeared in bit roles on *Casualty*, *Toast of London*, *Silent Witness*, and *Mr. Selfridge*.

When Daisy wasn't attending auditions, she spent time at the London flat that she shared with her sister. Usually, she relaxed on the sofa by knitting and watching *Netflix*. Her favorite television show? *House of Cards*. She adored the Kevin Spacey show about a ruthless politician. Sometimes the young woman played with her dog, Muffin, who happens to be deaf and blind.

In late 2013, Daisy heard from a friend that auditions had begun in London for the new *Star Wars* movie. In a highly-publicized transaction, Disney had purchased the rights to the galactic space opera and promptly enlisted J.J. Abrams to direct the franchise's first film in ten years. In other exciting news, original Star Wars leads, Mark Hamill, Carrie Fisher, and Harrison Ford, were all returning to their iconic roles as Luke Skywalker, Princess Leia, and Han Solo, respectively. In rounding out the cast, the director was also conducting extensive searches for young, unknown actors to join the famous series as new characters in *The Force Awakens*.

Although Daisy had grown up aware of the *Star Wars* phenomenon, she never considered herself a huge fan of the series. However, the actress knew that she needed to audition for the new movie.

"I immediately got this weird feeling all over my body," the actress told *Elle Magazine*. "I knew I had to be seen for it."

The persistent actress e-mailed her agent and asked for an audition. After several weeks passed, she finally received a phone call telling her she had a tryout for the movie. On the day of her first audition, Daisy waited in the lobby when director Abrams happened to walk by her. He noticed the waiting actress right away. At 5'7" with stunning good looks, she immediately stood out from the rest of the women. Could she act, though?

Abrams received his answer when Daisy slam dunked her audition. The actress delighted Abrams with her humor, grit, and spark. He called her back to read again and then three more times. After five auditions, she won the role of Rey, the story's central character, whose background remains a mystery. One crucial reading won her the role.

"I had her do a scene where she had to get pretty emotional, and she nailed it on the first take," Abrams revealed to *Elle Magazine*. "She was born with this gift

Daisy **Ridley**: Behind the Rebel

to be in a moment and make it her own. She simultaneously works from the inside out and the outside in."

Because *The Force Awakens'* details needed to remain a top secret, producers forbade its actors from discussing the movie, including its casting, with anyone. Daisy was on a date when her agent called to tell her she had won the part. Although the actress felt thrilled by the turn of events, she couldn't even share her astounding news with her date!

Daisy learned that *The Force Awakens* would not start filming right away. Because the role required enormous physicality, she would first spend three grueling months training for the movie. So, for five hours each day, five days a week, the young woman underwent stunt training and strength exercises at London's Pinewood Studios.

"J.J. wanted me to look stronger because I was pretty weedy," she told *The Times*. "There was a big emphasis on 'getting guns.'"

Eventually, Daisy confided to close family members about her big break. After all, they were starting to wonder why she was rarely around anymore. The caring young woman did not want anyone thinking she was purposefully avoiding them!

Soon, the rest of the world got word of Daisy's casting, too. On April 29, 2014, the entire *Star Wars:*

The Force Awakens principal cast assembled for their first table read of the heavily-guarded script at the historic Pinewood Studios located 20 miles west of London. The British movie and television studio has been the filming location for many famous movies over the years. *The Red Shoes* (1948), *The Prince and the Showgirl* (1957), *Fiddler on the Roof* (1971), *Superman* (1978), *Batman* (1989), *Love Actually* (2003), and numerous James Bond films were all shot there. It was also the memorable site of the original *Star Wars*.

At the read-through, Daisy almost pinched herself in disbelief. The excited actress found herself sitting between two major icons, Harrison Ford (Han Solo) and Carrie Fisher (Princess Leia). Was she actually filming a movie with them?

Ultimately, someone snapped a picture of the complete cast. Not surprisingly, the photograph quickly went viral. *Star Wars* enthusiasts spent hours analyzing the photo hoping to uncover even the smallest clues about the movie. Fans also bombarded *Google* searching for information on the unknown actress named Daisy Ridley!

Later that day, Daisy tweeted: "Overwhelmed by all the support. This is the greatest day of my life. I'm told I can't say who I'm playing yet, but it's exciting!"

"I'm not surprised she got this part," Donna

Hayward, director of her musical theater course at Tring, told *The Mirror*. "There was always something very special about her. She was always very feisty, but nicely feisty, very clever, independent. If she sets her mind on doing something she'll achieve it."

In addition to its original stars, John Boyega headlined the cast as a rogue Stormtrooper named Finn.

Meanwhile, Oscar Isaac, Adam Driver, and Andy Serkis also rounded out the roster. Several weeks later, Oscar-winner Lupita Nyong'o and *Game of Thrones'* Gwendoline Christie joined the lineup.

Daisy felt dazed on her first day of filming. The actress did not even have an actor page on *IMDB.com*, but now she was headlining the biggest movie franchise of all time. She felt like a bundle of nerves and began doubting her abilities.

"I was petrified," she told *Glamour Magazine*. "I thought I was gonna have a panic attack on the first day."

Early in the filming, Abrams told Daisy that her performance was "wooden." He knew his leading lady was capable of a much better performance. Rather than be offended by her director's assessment, the actress knew that his criticism was warranted. In the end, his words snapped her out of her funk and helped her to refocus.

"To be honest, I was struggling at that point, and he definitely brought out the best I could have possibly given," she explained to *Vogue*.

Daisy pulled her nerves together to show the stellar acting skills that had won her the part in the first place. It also helped that her veteran co-stars were supportive and down-to-earth. At one point during the shoot, she called Harrison Ford "Mr. Ford," and he insisted that she should call him by his first name. Additionally, Carrie Fisher took the young actress under her wing, offering her valuable advice.

Soon Daisy became quite comfortable on the film set. The actress even found herself singing and humming between takes. It's a habit that she doesn't even realize she's doing sometimes.

"Once J.J. bet me that I couldn't go a full day without singing — and I almost finished the day, and I started singing again," Daisy told *The Hollywood Reporter*.

At one point during the shooting, Daisy discovered that one of *The Force Awakens'* camera operators had worked on the movie, *Matilda*. The excited actress felt thrilled to meet someone who had been on the set of her favorite film. She spent an entire day inundating the man with questions about it!

Principal photography on *The Force Awakens* eventually ended on November 14, 2014. Disney scheduled the film for a December 18, 2015, opening. That meant Daisy Ridley had a year of anonymity before her face exploded everywhere.

"I think Rey is incredibly brave and hopeful and her story will be inspirational, and so for that, I'm thankful that I was able to play that."

On March 14, 2015, four blocks of Hollywood Boulevard shut down to accommodate the momentous world premiere of *Star Wars: The Force Awakens*. In true Hollywood fashion, Daisy arrived in a limousine surrounded by handlers. Fans, reporters, and photographers chanted, "Daisy, Daisy, Daisy" at first sight of her while camera flashes nearly blinded her.

To call the world premiere a smashing success would be an enormous understatement. Audiences hooted, hollered, applauded, and cried throughout the thrilling, 138-minute space adventure. Familiar faces were met with cheers, while new faces, like Daisy's, were enthusiastically welcomed into the *Star Wars* family.

Star Wars: The Force Awakens takes place thirty years after the Rebellion defeated the Galactic Empire. Luke Skywalker has vanished, and the galaxy faces a new danger from Supreme Leader Snoke and evil Kylo Ren. Can Leia Organa's military force, the Resistance, aided by Han Solo and his two new recruits, Rey and Fin, stop the latest threat of evil?

Rey's mysterious backstory provided much intrigue to *Star Wars* viewers. The scavenger with force skills grew up on the desert planet, Jakku, seemingly abandoned by her family as a child. Believing her loved ones will one day return, Rey befriends BB8, a small droid on a classified mission that barely escaped capture by the First Order. Along the way, she meets Finn, a Stormtrooper who has defected from the First Order, who pretends that he is with the Resistance. The humans and robot flee the planet on the deserted Millennium Falcon. From there, a tractor beam controlled by the legendary Han Solo and Chewbacca captures the ship. The smuggler and Wookiee agree to help the young couple return BB8 to the Resistance. Throughout her adventures, Rey forges friendships, suffers a loss, and battles the evil Kylo Ren in an epic lightsaber showdown.

When *The Force Awakens* opened, audiences swarmed theaters in record numbers. The film grossed 248 million dollars in its opening weekend alone. Overall, it earned 935 million dollars at the box office. Worldwide, the movie boasted over two billion dollars in ticket sales.

Critics were equally smitten with the latest *Star Wars* adventure. The film earned rave reviews with Daisy, John Boyega, and Harrison Ford earning the biggest kudos.

Dana Stevens from *Slate* gushed, "Boyega's Finn and Ridley's Rey are brave, funny, and admirable but also imperfect, uncertain, and sometimes afraid. That is to say, they're genuine, multisided characters with believable motivations."

Bruce Kirkland from the *Toronto Sun* wrote, "Ridley's Rey and Boyega's Finn give us a pair of dynamic new heroes to follow in future *Star Wars* Episodes."

"Ridley's spunky daredevil presence is exactly what the part calls for," praised Kenneth Turan of the *Los Angeles Times*.

Daisy turned up everywhere talking about *The Force Awakens*. She appeared on *Ellen, Conan, The Tonight Show Starring Jimmy Fallon, Jimmy Kimmel Live!, Saturday Night Live*, and more.

Additionally, Daisy attended her first Oscar ceremony. The excited actress co-presented Best Documentary Feature with actor Dev Patel at *The 88th Annual Academy Awards*. She looked stunning in an embroidered, silver blue Chanel Haute Couture dress.

She also graced several magazine covers. *Elle, Glamour, Style, Vanity Fair, People, The Hollywood Reporter, Entertainment Weekly*, and *Rolling Stone* were several publications that featured her prominently.

Being thrust into the spotlight can be an overwhelming experience for many. Fortunately, Daisy handled the newfound attention with grace and humor. Understandably, her parents were quite impressed with their successful daughter.

"I'm very proud of her and very glad for her," her father remarked. "There is no doubt she will be able to handle it. Emotionally she is very focused. She is an amazing and very inspiring person."

*"Dive in feet first.
Take everything you can and
appreciate every day."*

How does one follow the tremendous success of starring in the seventh *Star Wars* movie? How about starring in the eighth *Star Wars* film? Fans were thrilled when Daisy returned to her heralded role of Rey for the series' next installment, titled, *The Last Jedi*. Like the franchises' previous films, all involved in the production were ordered to keep the movie's details heavily guarded. Fans would see the Rian Johnson-directed film on December 15, 2017.

Meanwhile, Daisy had the opportunity to flaunt her acting muscles in a different kind of film when she joined the cast of *Murder on the Orient Express*. Directed by Kenneth Branagh, the film boasted an all-star roster. Johnny Depp, Michelle Pfeiffer, and Judi Dench were among the cast members.

The multitalented performer also returned to her singing roots when the legendary Barbra Streisand recruited her as a guest on her album *Encore: Movie Partners Sing Broadway*. The album's first track, "At the Ballet" from *A Chorus Line*, featured Daisy, Barbra, and Oscar winner Anne Hathaway playing the characters of Bebe, Sheila, and Maggie, respectively.

"I have had no experience recording so to have my first experience recording with Barbra Streisand is pretty insane," Daisy gushed.

"It was amazing!" she added. "She's an incredible human being."

Daisy didn't just record a Broadway song with the iconic superstar. She was also invited over to Barbra's home for tea. After the *Star Wars* actress had left her idol's house, she sat in her car and wept tears of happiness. A few days later, she even attended the Oscar-winner's concert.

Meanwhile, Daisy's film career continued to thrive. The busy actress had four films on the horizon that showcased her versatility. She secured the title role in *Ophelia*, a reimagining of *Hamlet* from the female perspective, a fantasy thriller co-starring Naomi Watts, a dystopian drama from Oscar-winning screenwriter Charlie Kaufman, a World War II drama, and the animated feature, *Peter Rabbit*.

Of course, there was also a little-known film called *The Last Jedi* on the horizon. Daisy would follow that movie by filming the ninth episode in the *Star Wars* series. The actress would be busy for some time, and that's how she liked it.

To many people, no matter what happens in the future, or how many awards she wins, Daisy will

always be the first major character she brought to life, Rey, the girl longing for a home in *The Force Awakens*. When asked to describe the character's journey, she may as well have been talking about herself.

"She is thrust into this adventure and reaches new possibilities and heights that she never believed she could have done," she told *refinery29.com*. "She's pushed beyond her limits; she meets people and forms relationships she never imagined was possible. And everything she does exceeds everything she could have ever imagined. It's a really wonderful story. She's just a young girl on a journey trying to do the right thing."

2016 Oscar Wilde Awards
Guillermo Proano / PR Photos

Jameson Empire Film Awards
Landmark / PR Photos

Star Wars: The Force Awakens World Premiere
Landmark / PR Photos

The Eagle Huntress Premiere in Los Angeles
PR Photos

Adam Driver & Daisy at the Star Wars: The Force Awakens Press Conference
Izumi Hasegawa / PR Photos

Daisy at the EE British Academy Film Awards
Landmark / PR Photos

ESSENTIAL LINKS

Official Websites
www.starwars.com

Facebook
www.facebook.com/DaisyRidleyOfficial

Twitter
@starwars

Instagram
www.instagram.com/starwars

Daisy with Stormtroopers
PR Photos

Creative Media Publishing has produced biographies on several inspiring personalities: *Simone Biles, Nadia Comaneci, Clayton Kershaw, Mike Trout, Yuna Kim, Shawn Johnson, Nastia Liukin, The Fierce Five, Gabby Douglas, Sutton Foster, Kelly Clarkson, Idina Menzel, Missy Franklin* and more. They've published two award-winning Young Adult novels, *Cutters Don't Cry* (Moonbeam Children's Book Award) and *Kaylee: The "What If?" Game* (Children's Literary Classic Awards). They have also produced a line of popular children's book series, including *The Creeper and the Cat, Future Presidents Club, Princess Dessabelle* and *Quinn: The Ballerina*.

www.CreativeMedia.net
@CMIPublishing

Now sports fans can learn about gymnastics' greatest stars! Americans **Shawn Johnson** and **Nastia Liukin** became the darlings of the 2008 Beijing Olympics when the fearless gymnasts collected 9 medals between them. Four years later at the 2012 London Olympics, America's **Fab Five** claimed gold in the team competition. A few days later, **Gabby Douglas** added another gold medal to her collection when she became the fourth American woman in history to win the Olympic all-around title. The *GymnStars* series reveals these gymnasts' long, arduous path to Olympic glory. *Gabby Douglas: Golden Smile, Golden Triumph* received a **2012 Moonbeam Children's Book Award**.

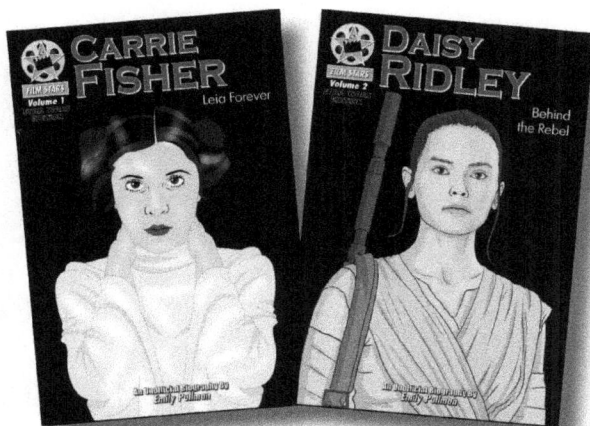

Before she was **Princess Leia** in *Star Wars*, **Carrie Fisher** was a young girl who loved to read and write and just happened to have famous parents. She never dreamed of being an actress like her mother, **Debbie Reynolds**, or a singer like her father, **Eddie Fisher**. When she auditioned for a sci-fi film on a whim, she had no idea it would change her life and turn her into a film icon. *Carrie Fisher: Leia Forever* is a biography for young readers who want to know more about the woman behind **Princess Leia**.

Our **YNot Girl** series chronicles the lives and careers of the world's most famous role models. ***Jennie Finch: Softball Superstar*** details the California native's journey from a shy youngster to softball's most famous face. In ***Kelly Clarkson: Behind Her Hazel Eyes***, young readers will find inspiration reading about the superstar's rise from a broke waitress with big dreams to becoming one of the recording industry's top musical acts. ***Missy Franklin: Swimming Sensation*** narrates the Colorado native's transformation from a talented swimming toddler to queen of the pool.

After her triumphant turn as *Thoroughly Modern Millie*, Sutton Foster charmed Broadway audiences by playing a writer, a princess, a movie star, a nightclub singer, and a Transylvania farm girl. A children's biography, **Sutton Foster: Broadway Sweetheart, TV Bunhead** details the role model's rise from a tiny ballerina to the toast of Broadway.

Idina Menzel's career has been "Defying Gravity" for years! With starring roles in *Wicked* and *Rent*, the Tony-winner filmed a recurring role on *Glee* and lent her talents to the Disney films, *Enchanted* and *Frozen*. A children's biography, **Idina Menzel: Broadway Superstar** narrates the actress' rise to fame!

Get ready to chase your dreams after reading this thrilling children's biography on *Hamilton* creator **Lin-Manuel Miranda**. A terrific source for a book report, **Lin-Manuel Miranda: Lights Up** tells the inspiring life story of the role model's transformation from a young boy with Broadway dreams to one of today's most respected artists.

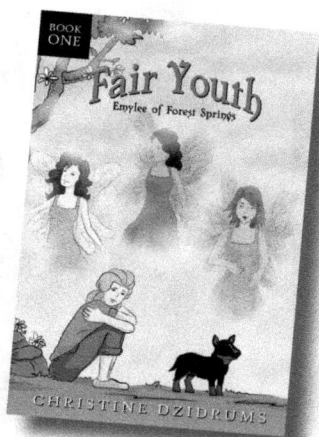

Twelve-year-old Emylee Markette has felt invisible her entire life. Then one fateful afternoon, three beautiful sisters arrive in her sleepy New England town and instantly become the most popular girls at Forest Springs Middle School. To everyone's surprise, the Fay sisters befriend Emylee and welcome her into their close-knit circle. Before long, the shy loner finds herself running with the cool crowd, joining the track team and even becoming friends with her lifelong crush.

Through it all, though, Emylee's weighed down by nagging suspicions. Why were the Fay sisters so anxious to befriend her? How do they know some of her inner thoughts? What do they truly want from her?

When Emylee eventually discovers that her new friends are secretly fairies, she finds her life turned upside down yet again and must make some life-changing decisions.

Fair Youth: Emylee of Forest Springs marks the first volume in an exciting new book series.

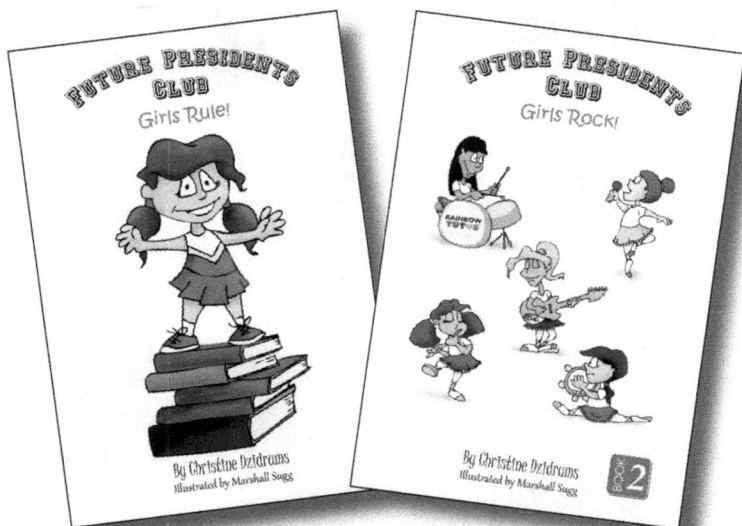

Ashley Moore wants to know why there's never been a girl president. Before long the inspired six-year-old creates a special, girls-only club - the **Future Presidents Club**. Meet five enthusiastic young girls who are ready to change the world. *Future Presidents Club: Girls Rule* is the first book in a series about girls making a difference!

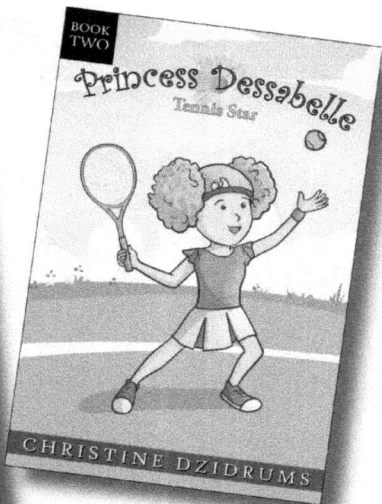

Meet **Princess Dessabelle**, a spoiled, lonely princess with a quick temper.

In *Princess Dessabelle Makes a Friend*, the lonely youngster discovers the meaning of true friendship. *Princess Dessabelle: Tennis Star* finds the pampered girl learning the importance of good sportsmanship.

Quinn
The Ballerina
The Sleeping Beauty

ʙʏCHRISTINE **DZIDRUMS**

Quinn the Ballerina can hardly believe it's finally performance day. She's playing her first principal role in a production of *The Sleeping Beauty*.

Yet, Quinn is also nervous. Can she really dance the challenging steps? Will people believe her as a cursed princess caught in a 100-year spell?

Join Quinn as she transforms into Princess Aurora in an exciting retelling of Tchaikovsky's *The Sleeping Beauty*. Now you can relive, or experience for the first time, one of ballet's most acclaimed works as interpreted by a 9 year old.

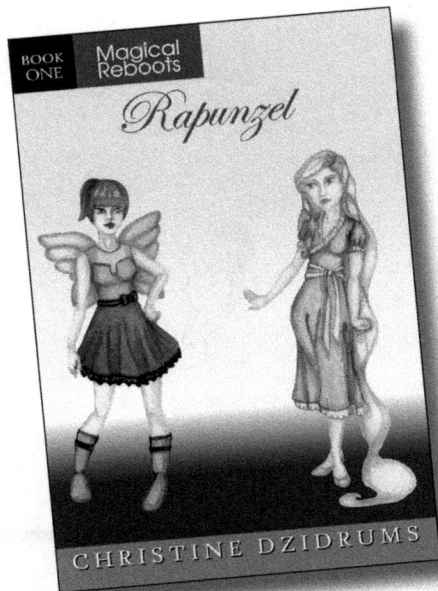

From the popular new series, ***Classical Reboots,*** *Rapunzel* updates the **Brothers Grimm** fairy tale with hilarious and heartbreaking results.

Rapunzel has been locked in her adoptive mother's attic for years. Just as the despondent teenager abandons hope of escaping her private prison, a mysterious tablet computer appears. Before long, Rapunzel's quirky fairy godmother, Aiko, has the conflicted young girl questioning her place in the world.

Cutters Don't Cry
2010 Moonbeam Children's Book Award Winner! In a series of raw journal entries written to her absentee father, a teenager chronicles her penchant for self-harm, a serious struggle with depression and an inability to vocally express her feelings.

Kaylee: The 'What If?' Game
"I play the 'What If?'" game all the time. It's a cruel, wicked game."

When free spirit Kaylee suffers a devastating loss, her personality turns dark as she struggles with depression and un-resolved anger. Can Kaylee repair her broken spirit, or will she remain a changed person?

www.ingramcontent.com/pod-product-compliance
Lightning Source LLC
Chambersburg PA
CBHW071645040426
42452CB00009B/1767